THE PUBLIC SERVANTS'

SURVIVAL

GUIDE

10 KEYS TO RECLAIM
YOUR JOY IN WORK &
LIFE WHILE DOING
WHAT YOU LOVE

BRENDA J. VIOLA

Writing & Publishing Process by
PlugAndPlayPublishing.com

Book Cover by Jillian Hampson/SlyCatDesign

Edited by Jenny Butterfield

ISBN: 9781673277128

To Mark, with your kindness and support,
you are the steady turtle to my hare.

Acknowledgements

This book could not exist without the memories created during my years in public service.

My comrades in arms who helped me survive – and thrive - during my decade as a Public Information Officer (PIO) must be named: Eileen Trainer (Lucy to my Ethel), Doug Cleland, Pat Ryan, Bob Duncan, Mary Graham-Zak, Chief Chas McGarvey, Superintendent Joe Daly, the late Chief Harry Knorr, Superintendent Mike McGrath, Lindsay Taylor, Tom Pintande, Chris Steckel, Dean Dortone, Gilbert P. High, Lori Jennings, Gina Pellicciotta, and my sisters from other mothers, Roseann McGrath and Jody Kelley.

A special thanks to Don Cannon, who inspired me to give my first public workshop on "Mastering the Media" to the American Public Works Association in 2009.

And another special thanks to Sue Hann who approached me after that first workshop and said, "Everyone needs to hear this."

Heartfelt thanks to every one of the 500+ municipal workers with whom I was privileged to serve during my tenure.

Amy Brewer and the Florida Association of City Clerks asked me to create a keynote in 2014, which provided the framework for this book. I owe the FACC a debt of gratitude. This organization urged me to reach out to Ashley DiBlasi at the International Municipal Clerks Association, launching my speaking career to new heights. What can I say? Clerks – you ROCK!

As do Planners. And Librarians. And Teachers. Police and Firefighters, Public Works and Parks and Recreation employees. Managers and Administrators. CFO's, CIO's, PIO's and of course, elected officials. This book is for you.

Because we can't afford good people to burn out and stop serving.

Our communities need you.

You matter.

There's nothing more rewarding than being a part of a great team, and I must acknowledge the leadership and inspiration received from my private sector colleagues at Medical Solutions Supplier. From Steve and Renee Kantor, the greatest friends and owners that ever started a company, to Joseph Carberry, who shows up in remarkable ways to make life better for everyone he encounters, to my Exec Team family: Debbi Lalli, Cynthia Harcourt, Ed Davis, Tony Purcell, Kathy Viola, and Gary Welsh – your expertise and insight, curiosity and kindness have made me better, personally and professionally.

Angela Pointon, new and dear friend, thank you for the nudge to work with coach Weston Lyon. And to the generous and energetic California Clerk Stephanie Smith, thank you for e-mailing me after a session to say, "You must write a book." To my "bookie" friend, Cindy O'Krepki: thank you for planting a seed with our collaboration on *Lifelong Looper* many years ago.

Eric Ansart, thank you for being my volcano-building partner and brother all these years.

To my "go-to" tribe, the magical, amazing, kind, and generous besties Anita Hampson, Cynthia

Harcourt, and Renee Kantor. Thank you for talking me down from every ledge and raising me up from every valley. We four are truly fab.

Shirlee DiBacco, having you for a sister has made all the difference. And mom? Well, you're the best.

As my favorite quote about public service (and life) goes – a mash-up between Teddy Roosevelt and the fictional Leslie Knope from **Parks and Recreation**: "The best prize life has to offer is a chance to work hard at work worth doing. And I would add that what makes work worth doing is getting to do it with people you love." How true this is!

Table of Contents

Read This First

After a decade of service in municipal government, my sense of enthusiasm for public service waned.

It wasn't the work itself. Few things are more fulfilling than leading projects that directly impact the quality of life in a community. Long after the pillar employees of municipal, county, state, and federal government retire, the roads they paved, the parks they maintained, the policies they created, the elections they oversaw, the open records they provided, and the library book selections they curated remain.

This is legacy work.

Serving makes a difference because public service impacts human beings where they live – literally.

The work energizes, but the demands of these jobs could drain even the most resilient of workers.

In my experience, public meetings for government debate and discussion usually started at 6:30 PM and extended into the wee hours of the morning, only to return at 8:15 AM the next day. On meeting nights, the hours passed to offer each elected official their say. With gavel-to-gavel coverage provided by the community's government access channel, each Commissioner vied for camera time, extending what could have been a fifteen-minute discussion into many hours of repetitive oratory.

Staff members respectfully sat as the hours passed, poised to respond if called upon. How glad I was that the citizens in attendance and the Commissioners seated on stage couldn't read our minds. It's not that we wished to squelch public discourse. We simply wanted to go HOME for a real dinner or finally cheer on the sidelines at our child's sporting events.

Beyond the televised public meetings, there was a constant stream of ribbon cuttings, groundbreaking ceremonies, parlor meetings, civic association gatherings, and advisory committee sessions that extended the workday well beyond eight hours.

The time involved was clearly tiring, but perhaps the scrutiny and disdain from the very public we served was most grueling. Don't get me wrong. There were far more kind and appreciative citizens than faultfinders. Still, when you've put in several consecutive twelve-hour days and a disgruntled resident reminds you that he or she "is paying your salary," that spiteful reminder tends to deplete what energy remains.

My decade as a Public Information Officer included coaching elected officials and municipal leaders to excel at media inquiries. The ability to deftly answer reporters' questions and use their platforms to educate and inform was a critically important skill I enjoyed teaching.

In 2009, the American Public Works Association issued a call for presentations which inspired me to create my "Mastering the Media" workshop. At the end of my session, an attendee approached me and said, "You should do more of this. People need to hear what you have to say."

With no marketing and solely word of mouth recommendations, my speaking business grew, as did my course offerings. Developing material was easy because the ideas were born from my first-hand experience. As I stood before audiences – from the American Library Association to the International Institute of Municipal Clerks – I observed that they all had something in common.

They were burned out.

These annual conferences were their one big chance to refuel, recharge, and be reminded of WHY they got into public service in the first place.

They were super busy taking care of business, but in many cases, these public servants weren't taking care of *themselves*.

How could I impart a message that could help sustain these dedicated people after the closing ceremony?

That's when the ***Public Servants' Survival Guide*** was born.

I'm proud to say that the material contained in the following pages provides a framework for avoiding burnout and recommendations to help you course correct. Those of you who are brave enough to honestly answer the questions posed are poised for a breakthrough rather than a breakdown.

Further, those of you who not only realized you are imbalanced, but are also taking action to make a change, are to be applauded.

You may or may not be the City Manager or Board President, but you *are* the CEO of your own life. Taking care of you will be the smartest thing you will ever do. And taking care of yourself will restore your joy in work AND in life.

I'm rooting for you!

How to Get the Most Out of This Book

I'm sure somewhere along the line you've read *Aesop's Fable*, "The Tortoise and the Hare." I love that story for many reasons! However, in this book, I want to give you a different version of this famous tale.

Instead of the Turtle and the Hare being at odds, I see them working together and encouraging each other to be their best. And they *both* win.

Public service is a demanding, grueling, and often thankless profession. It can sometimes feel like an unwinnable race. So, to help you along your journey, I've designed this survival guide with ten chapters to offer insight and perspective. A playbook to navigate your career in public service! The first letters of the first six chapters spell out T-U-R-T-L-E, and the first letters of the last four chapters spell out H-A-R-E.

Think about the people in your world. Putting them into just two buckets would be impossible (and wrong). However, I've found that temperaments lean toward either a Turtle or a Hare.

Turtles are deliberate and intentional, slower and methodical. Sometimes you don't know what they're thinking because they think a matter fully through before talking. Averse to risk-taking, they plot their course and don't take a step before crossing all the t's and dotting all the i's.

Hares can be impulsive, but their flashes of brilliance can electrify a meeting or take a project to new heights. When inspired, they take action. They leave everyone else in the dust but can arrive completely unprepared for the challenges that await them.

Each temperament has its gifts as well as its drawbacks. Often the best couples or the best teams are comprised of this yin and yang, and sometimes we display the characteristics of both, depending on the situation.

You might be drawn to retreat into your turtle shell to ponder solutions to a problem. Or you might surprise everyone in the room with a shocking, out-of-the-box idea that involves risk and the potential for great reward. Do you see yourself as predominantly one temperament or the other? Or a balance of each?

My hope is that by working together with both the Turtle and the Hare, this book will help you win your race and reclaim the joy in your life and in your work. Remember, the goal is not to just survive but to *thrive*!

Your Survival Guide Self-Assessment

As public servants, we're constantly asked to go the extra mile. But as you know, going the extra mile when you're running on empty is impossible. That's why I've created a self-assessment to help you see where you are.

Each chapter that follows will end with a chance for you to grade yourself.

The scale is simple: a score of ten means that you are a rock star, absolute perfection in this category. Zero acknowledges complete and utter failure in this category. In most cases, you'll hover between four and seven with one or two categories where you shine.

There are ten main categories. At the end, you'll tally your scores from each. And here's what your total indicates:

90 - 100: Why are you even reading this book? You should be the one writing this book! Now subtract five points for smugness. (Only kidding!)

80 - 90: You have a healthy level of self-awareness and are probably one pedicure or round of golf away from being refreshed to go the extra mile.

70 - 80: Time to schedule a night out with your best friends and get a good night's sleep. Immediately!

60 - 70: Stop trying to be Wonder Woman or Superman! You need help, some go-to people, a vacation, and probably a martini or a huge cookie.

Under 60: You need a hug (and possibly a visit

to the emergency room.) Or a vacation. Time to start taking care of YOU.

This Is Between You and You

Would it be a good idea for a trusted colleague to fill out the assessment on your behalf? Perhaps an objective party could provide insights into blind spots you might overlook?

You could go that route, but it's not my recommendation. This is between you and you. Only *you* know if you've been drinking an entire bottle of red wine at night to cope with work and home stress. Only *you* know if you stare at the ceiling at 3 AM, filled with anxiety about a meeting you're dreading. And only *you* can remember the last time you had a belly laugh instead of fuming with anger.

If you'll be brave enough to honestly answer the questions raised, you can determine the next steps that feel right to you.

I'm never a fan of other people getting up in my business. Yes, I value coaching and assistance from my team and leaders to help me prioritize, improve, and achieve the objectives of our organization. But the real juice of the information in this book is deeply personal. I'm a strong believer that the quality of your inner life equates to the quality of your personal and professional lives. Get *that* in alignment and good stuff will follow!

Are you ready to get started? In the next chapter, we'll start our journey together with the Turtle and talk about teamwork.

TURTLE
Teamwork

"It takes two to make a thing go right…"
– Salt-n-Pepa

My first, big challenge as a Public Information Officer (PIO) was handling the hoopla for a much-scrutinized, half-a-million-dollar township signage project. Colorful banners would be hung throughout the township noting each historical district – the first time our community had invested in such fancy branding.

Making flyers, inviting the press, issuing press releases, and scripting remarks were all part of the big reveal, and I relished each task.

Well, each task except for *one*.

How the banners would actually roll open for a big reveal kept me awake at night.

The plan was to unveil the signage to the public with a "ta-da" flourish. "Ooohs" and "aaaahs" would ensue. The crowd would erupt into applause. Action News would capture 30 seconds for the evening news. And the tension surrounding my PIO probationary period would vanish.

Except, I had no budget for fancy mechanics or pyrotechnics. And for the life of me, I couldn't figure out how I could get a darned sign to roll open from the street pole vantage point, 15 feet above us all. As the big day drew near, the pit in my stomach grew exponentially. I was at a complete loss.

At the end of my rope, I shared my angst with my roommate.

Helen, by the way, has horrible grammar and would rather have root canal than script a special event or speak in public. She does, however, possess her own set of power tools, she actually reads and follows Ikea instructions, and she can figure out mechanical mysteries in a flash.

Mind you, I was just looking for a sympathetic ear, not expecting a solution.

I shared my worst-case scenario: a boring, no-flourish photo op with an open banner flapping unceremoniously in the breeze. I also shared my elusive dream: a perfectly on-cue, dramatic un-veiling preceded by a drumroll.

Helen left the room and returned with two black binder clips. You know, the kind found in any office drawer with the silver ends you squeeze to open and close the grip? Then she rolled up a piece of paper, securing it at each end with the clips. Next, she snipped two long strings of rib-bon, tying one to each clip.

The fog lifted. I got the vision!

And ribbon is cheap! It can be cut any length you want (yes, even the 15+ feet needed for this pro-ject). The Board President and Vice-President could each clutch a ribbon end, and at the count of 3...2...1..., simultaneously tug. The clips would break away and gloriously reveal the banner as imagined in my dreams.

Oh, yes! The reveal was a smashing, low-budget success. But more valuable than the good press was the lesson learned about not being a lone ranger.

What Do You Like and What Do You Loathe?

Why do we waste so much time and energy on tasks not in our wheelhouse? For me, I desperately sought to prove that my employer hadn't made a mistake hiring me. Somehow, asking for help seemed a sign of weakness. Dare I let them think I *didn't* know it all?

Insecurity, pride, doubt, ego... take your pick. These are simply disguising the true culprit: fear. And fear is the great diminisher. When we let fear win the day, it causes us to retreat into our turtle shells and shrink back from collaboration. If the Turtle in the classic fable had listened to fear, he *never* would have taken on the Hare.

Embracing the opposite – LOVE – expands your world, invites help, shares the success, and builds partnerships.

When we don't ask for help, we're voting with fear. We pinch ourselves off from the abundant flow of solutions available to us.

"When we don't ask for help, we're voting with fear."

Asking for assistance will *never* diminish you. And people love to help! Pitching in, solving problems, and contributing makes people feel great.

One of the world's great sales trainers, Jack Daly, encourages his audiences to focus on Highly Profitable Activities (HPA's). This concept translates beautifully to any kind of work.

The question to be asked is, "What am I spending time on that I hate or simply stink at doing?"

These are the tasks that zap your energy, steal your joy, and cause you to hate coming in to work in the morning.

I recommend that you write a Like/Loathe List.

What are the tasks that light you up? These aspects of your job are more like fun than work to you because you're good at them.

What do you dread doing? Give me a paragraph to proofread, and that task is like candy to me. Ask me to tally up numbers and create a spreadsheet? I get an instant migraine.

But someone out there gets a charge out of a pivot table.

Take a moment right now and write *your* Like/Loathe List.

LIKE	LOATHE
1.	1.
2.	2.
3.	3.
4.	4.
5.	5.
6.	6.
7.	7.
8.	8.
9.	9.
10.	10.

Too often we spend time banging our heads against the wall, doing stuff we have no business doing and never reaching out to see if the person in the next cubicle might *love* that thing you *loathe.*

No One Likes to Iron! Right?

My dear mom, Bette, had a sweet, little job handing out coupons at the local BJ's Wholesale Club.

Just two days a week, this job gave her a reason to get up, do her hair, and interact with people – something she longed for after retirement.

One day, the manager called her into the office and said, "Bette, you are a wonderful asset to our team. But I am sorry to say that the coupon position is being discontinued."

There are few things more distressing than seeing your 80-year-old mom cry.

My sister and I were at a loss. What could we do to make her happy again?

Finally, we asked her, "Mom. What would you *like* to do?"

She sat silently for several moments and considered the question. She looked up, eyes red from tears and said, "I really like to iron."

Iron?

No one likes to iron!

But my mom finds ironing relaxing. So, we created the flyer on page 22 for my mom.

We often find it mind-boggling that someone could love the very thing we loathe. Sometimes, a simple conversation can reveal the hidden talents hiding around the next cubicle.

Wouldn't you be energized by offloading even *one* of those tasks on your Loathe List?

And take this beyond the work setting.

When you finally get a break, you've got to make the most of your down time. Too often we do what we've always done and never consider outsourcing.

Recently, when moving from an apartment to my home, the apartment needed to be fully cleaned so I could get my security deposit back.

Let Our Mom Iron for YOU!

Our Mom, Bette Costello, is the world's best ironer. She is not only an amazing ironer, she actually LIKES to do it.

We've been encouraging her to find some fun activities to get involved with...

...she's not interested.

But just last week she said, "You know what would make me happy? Doing other people's ironing. I could just go to their house and play some music and iron away."

What she wanted to charge was ridiculous, so we are suggesting $15 an hour. Think of how much time it will save you (and probably money, too!) She's better than any dry cleaner.

Plus, you'll make her happy. And nothing makes daughters happy than when their mom is happy.

She is only going to take on five clients, so call her soon!

Above is the flyer we created for my 80-year-old mom when she was laid off from her part-time job.

The idea of spending a Saturday cleaning (when I was up to my ears in boxes at the new place) made me downright depressed. I never thought that I could just hire someone for an hour or two to do what I dreaded, ensuring that I'd get my deposit (and my Saturday!)

The suggestion gave me pause. Why spend money when I could clean myself?

But how much was being happy and free on a Saturday worth to me?

As the Mastercard commercial says: PRICELESS.

The money spent on those cleaners was money well spent.

Let the people who enjoy eliminating dust bunnies take care of yours.

Let the whizzes in accounting make your spreadsheet tables while you proofread their paragraphs.

Let's start outsourcing, collaborating, and becoming team players.

Teachers and Teamwork

Every year, my cousin, Pam, struggles to equip her special-needs, public classroom with required supplies. Like many teachers, she often pulls out her own debit card to bridge the gap.

This year, she did something remarkably obvious, scathingly brilliant, and super-effective. She posted her "Back to School" wish list on her personal Facebook page. Her friends and family clamored to meet the need. Within twenty-four hours, every item had been purchased in multiples. Not only did the children benefit, we all felt great about pitching in. And Pam's heart was encouraged by the outpouring of support.

Imagine if the Turtle and the Hare had teamed up! The Rabbit could race to the riverbank, carrying the Turtle. And crossing a river? No problem for a Hare riding on the back of a Tortoise. Playing to each other's strengths and using situational leadership would win the race for *both* of them. (And a whole lot faster, too.)

Consider how much or how little you know about your co-workers' skills and interests. Consider your circle of friends and what they might offer if you just asked.

If you're drawing a blank, know that there's likely a boatload of opportunity to address your loathe list.

On a scale of 1 – 10, how do you rate yourself on Teamwork? Turn to page 151, and fill in your score.

TURTLE
Unity

"There is no strength without unity."
- Irish Proverb

My Facebook life looked AMAZING. Smiling with my husband in front of the Eiffel Tower. Our toes stretched out on sandy beaches facing the sea. Photo-worthy meals at high-end restaurants. Who could doubt I lived a dream life?

Only *I* knew what a facade my fake smiles were. In moments of reflection, these photos reminded me of the true back stories – the put-downs, disappointments, and heartbreaks preceding the photo ops.

"Approaching life as a performance will wear you out."

I was two people. The Brenda that everyone observed as the life of the party. The eternal optimist with a perpetual smile on her face. And the Brenda that cried herself to sleep because she knew she was miserably unhappy.

Pretending to be something or someone that you are not is exhausting. Approaching life as a performance will wear you out.

Work in public service for any length of time, and you'll realize that unifying *other* people is like herding cats. You'll never get everyone to agree about everything. Just getting people into the same room at the same time is hard enough!

I can tell you from experience that the fast track to wearing yourself out is to try and unify others or fix someone else.

So to be clear, in this chapter, I'm not talking about fixing someone else. The key to personal and professional fulfillment that I speak of here is the unity of your *own* body, soul, and spirit.

This is between you… and you.

Nourishing Your Body

Let's start with taking care of your body. Your external, physical layer needs to have food. Real food, not those orange crackers stored in the lunchroom closet that have been there for way too long. I should know. I used to snack on those crackers regularly, especially when late-night meetings ran well beyond the dinner hour.

In addition, your body requires exercise. When I worked in local government, I never took the one flight of steps up to my office. I always chose the elevator and rarely went to the gym after a grueling day. Give me the couch, some comfort food, and a mindless TV show to wipe the memory of the day away!

One of my favorite commercials, "Diva," features the legendary Aretha Franklin on a road trip with a group of millennials. She's complaining about the heat, kicking the seat in front of her, and generally being cranky. Her backseat companion hands her a Snickers bar, and after one bite, she turns back into their millennial friend. The tag line, "You're not you when you're hungry" says it all.

Don't miss breakfast AND lunch, and then try to be sharp at an important meeting. Some of you miss dinner too and wonder why you're at a breaking point!

If your nerves are frayed and your patience level is low, chances are you missed a meal. Sometimes you're a meal away from a better day.

Soothing Your Soul

Your soul is your mind, your will, and your emotions.

Too often, we live on autopilot and never tune in to what we are really thinking or feeling. "I have too much to get done to spend time looking inward!" is often our excuse.

We live as if on a conveyor belt, progressing to the famous Lucy and Ethel scene where they shove chocolates into their mouths, bras, and hats to appear to "keep up."

But you can only pretend so long that everything is okay before you reach a breaking point. The purpose of this chapter is to head off your breakdown at the pass. After all, while you pretend and perform to keep everyone else happy, you neglect your own inner being and rob yourself of living an authentic life.

The key is to place more value on how *you* feel about you and your life than what *others* think about you and your life. In addition, the only way to get from where you are to where you want to be is to learn how to process your feelings. Let your emotions and feelings have some room to breathe.

In fact, I suggest you tend to your emotions as you would a garden. Pay attention to your emotional garden. Prune the plants, and pull the weeds. Fertilize the soil, and watch your garden flourish.

Feelings aren't right or wrong – they're just the way you feel. So, learn to *feel* your emotions. Embrace them. And let them direct you to what's really going on so that you can pull out the weeds that are choking your joy at the root.

Left unattended, a garden will be overtaken with weeds, and the fruit of your labor will soon disappear. The same is true for your emotional garden. Left unattended, your emotions will spin out of control, leading to inappropriate out-

"Sometimes you're a meal away from a better day."

bursts and actions that can harm both your personal life and your professional credibility.

At a recent seminar, a former City Manager recalled putting up with a cantankerous Board for many years. He was met with resistance at every turn. Each initiative he tried to shepherd to completion was criticized in public meetings. Finally, he'd had enough. During a live, televised council meeting he stormed out, not realizing the door would lock behind him with his car keys, wallet, and cell phone out of reach in the room behind him. He can laugh about that situation now and we all joined in, but what a great example of allowing emotions to build to a literal point of no return.

Peel back those emotions, and you'll find their root in the thoughts you've been thinking. If fertilized by negative imaginings, a little thought like, "My boss doesn't listen to me" will grow to, "My boss hates me and is out to get me. I bet I'm going to be fired!"

If you feel sad, angry, dejected, hopeless, or anything other than happy, I guarantee those emotions are related to the thoughts you're entertaining.

Imagine your doorbell rings. You peek to see who's there, and for the sake of this story, Charles Manson is at your door. Would you open up, welcome him in, put on a pot of coffee, and usher him into the guest room?

Certainly not!

So, if we won't entertain people who are hurtful and damaging, why do we entertain thoughts that are hurtful, disruptive, draining, fearful, or any enemy of our happiness?

"But my boss IS a jerk! My workload IS impossible! My life IS a mess!"

Yep.

And the more energy you give to how you think about a situation, negative or positive, will determine how the situation progresses from here.

I'm not suggesting lying to yourself, but you can choose a thought that feels better to help soothe your emotions. "I am a good worker. Everything always gets done eventually. My life has challenges, but here's where it's beautiful..."

Try tuning into the positive instead. You'll feel better before you know it.

Your emotions are your internal guidance system. They let you know when you're "on" or "off" which is why ignoring them can be so damaging. Listen to them, peel back the feelings to the thoughts that provoked them, and often, you can pivot back to a place of peace.

Let me tell you about a difficult situation from my own life to illustrate my point. After fourteen years of suppressing my emotions and painting a happy but false picture of my marriage and begging for relationship counseling only to have my pleas met with, "If you don't like it, leave… ."

Well, after all that emotional inauthenticity, I finally arrived at a point of no return.

Friends came over for a barbecue, and we cooled off in the pool. My husband thought it would be funny to spray me, point blank, with his new pressure washer. The situation was humiliating; both physically and emotionally painful.

That water pounding in my face was the straw that broke the camel's back. After years of excusing injustices and contorting myself to uncover what I needed to change about *me* to make our marriage work, the pressure washer was a seminal moment. A tipping point.

When I went to Zumba class the next morning, the warmup song was Twisted Sister's "We're Not Gonna Take It." The song was an odd choice for this Pitbull-inclined crowd, but as I jumped and stretched the words sunk to a place in my psyche – my soul – that suddenly clicked.

I'm not gonna take it anymore.

No, I'm not gonna take it!

Suddenly, my beautiful house and my exotic vacations and gourmet meals meant NOTHING.

What mattered was peace.

This began the unification of Brenda. No more fake smiles for the camera. No more pretending.

This story could have ended a few different ways depending on how my husband responded, but let's just say he is now my ex-husband. And I wish him well.

You can spend your entire life trying to make others happy, but the only person you can ever really make happy is you.

Instead of ignoring those feelings behind the curtain, I now place a high priority on thinking good-feeling thoughts and on surrounding myself with people who don't expect me to perform for them.

Think about your day and the many different roles you play. At home, you may be mom or dad, husband or partner or roommate. At work, the Clerk or City Manager or Chief Fire Officer.

Your variety of hats include your civic, social, and other obligations.

Consider this interesting exercise.

Think about the predominant feelings you feel in each of these roles that you play.

Make a list under each, and consider the various roles and moods associated with each:

HOME	WORK	PLAY
1.	1.	1.
2.	2.	2.
3.	3.	3.
4.	4.	4.
5.	5.	5.

"Tend to your emotional guidance system as you would a garden."

Are patterns emerging? Is there a balance of both good and bad feelings under each? Or, is there a strong negative or positive emotional weight that overrides the total experience?

The point? You can't course correct if you're not *aware* of what you're feeling. Some of what you wrote in the lists on page 39 may have surprised you! The good news is, if you are conscious of the emotional temperature, you can adjust to create a better environment.

Tend to your emotional guidance system as you would a garden.

Doing so will bring balance, peace, and authenticity to each role you play. And best of all? You're not playing or performing. You're just being wonderful you.

Calming Your Spirit

No matter your belief system, whether you consider yourself spiritual or not, spirit is your very essence. Your spirit is the you-est you. The part untainted by the shrapnel of life. The purest you that embodies all that is good and right.

Your inner being is always emanating love and light, like an unsinkable cork that can't be submerged despite the crashing waves of life.

We can, however, choose to hold our inner being down. We each have our own special way of blocking the flow. Easily offended? Triggered to anger? Jealousy... complaining... playing the victim or the martyr?

What's *your* poison?

I now live in a smaller house with a wonderful man who is unfailingly kind. That kindness is healing some of the old wounds, and my soul is restored to a place where I focus more on things of spirit.

A canopy of trees surrounds our back deck, and my job is to pressure wash the debris. (Interesting how pressure washers keep showing up in my life? Therapists out there, feel free to weigh in!)

This process of shooting water at leaves, twigs, and dead bugs is actually a relaxing task, and watching the debris spin off out of view is meditative.

One day, about halfway through the job, the water suddenly stopped flowing. I pointed the nozzle at my face, looked around quizzically, and couldn't figure what the problem was. Until I followed the hose and saw a kink in the line.

One move to straighten the hose resulted in a gushing flow. I was back in business!

A thought occurred to me. That's how *life* is. The flow of spirit – the spirit that is the very core of you and me – is ever present. We sometimes get twisted up, and it appears that the well has run dry. But if we take time to unpack – or backtrack – we can see where we got the hose twisted.

Which is really the point of this chapter.

On a scale of 1 – 10, when you consider Unity in your life – body, soul, and spirit – how do you grade yourself? Turn to page 151, and fill in your score.

TURTLE
Rest

"Almost everything will work if you unplug it
for a few minutes. Including you."
– Anne Lamott

A re you a member of the 3 AM club? While the rest of the world sleeps peacefully or snores loudly, you're staring at the ceiling. You dare to look at your phone to see what time it is. And your heart sinks.

Your mind is alert, but you know by lunchtime your body will protest your lack of sleep. Still, you fiddle through Facebook and Instagram – maybe even find a Words with Friends player and try to feel tired.

You finally fall into a beautiful, deep sleep... five minutes before your alarm goes off.

Volumes have been written about how important sleep is to quality of life, and you already know the practical steps to take to ensure your body is getting rest.

My goal in this chapter is not to talk to you about a good night's sleep or taking a nap (though I strongly encourage both). Instead, my aim is to ask you to consider if you are "at rest" in how you live life as a whole.

Rest in peace shouldn't just be for dead people.

And resting doesn't necessarily mean lying horizontally with your eyes closed.

Taking a break from electronic devices. Really being off from work when you're out of the office. And actually TAKING a sick day instead of plowing through and gifting your co-workers with your workaholic germs. These are all important to rest.

There is also rest in your *soul* that is equally important.

"Rest in peace shouldn't just be for dead people."

When Life Gives You Lemons...

On a recent excursion to see the stunning Red Rocks in Arizona, my friend and I headed out in our rental car, excited to explore. At our first stop light, BOOM!

Yep, we'd been rear-ended. Fortunately, neither of us was injured. But we had to pull over, call 9-1-1, share insurance information, and wait for the paramedics to check us out.

No, this wasn't my idea of a grand evening in Sedona. But a thought occurred to me that we could either let the experience ruin our night, or we could approach this experience as an adventure. A little detour that, if approached with some good humor, could be inconsequential.

What you focus on in life gets bigger. The energy we give to complaints or injustices amplifies their power.

Similarly, if you seek the silver lining (gee, that EMT has the prettiest, blue eyes!), gratitude will grow.

A mind marinated in gratitude cannot coexist with turmoil.

Trials and tribulations are a fact of life. Peace is a choice. Will I side with the drama? Or calmly observe the chaos, realizing, "This too shall pass."

You know what? It always passes. Too often, I've given the stuff that hit the fan WAY too much of my time and energy.

If getting upset would help, I'd get upset. Worry, fear, anxiety, stress – none of these ever add value to a situation.

Now I must confess, I've only really lived a drama-free life for the last couple of years after a lifetime of being a full-blown exaggerator.

Something about milking the bad times, reenacting dramatic scenarios, raising my voice, and crying sloppy tears appealed to me. I'm a recovering performer.

This propensity for extreme, emotional outbursts was compounded during my marriage. My ex-husband's *inside* voice was like most children's *recess* volume.

We didn't talk. We screamed. Our house was so filled with turmoil that something had to give.

"A mind marinated in gratitude cannot coexist with turmoil."

For fourteen years, I begged that we get counseling together. For fourteen years, I heard in response, "If you don't like it, leave."

Like I mentioned earlier, when I went to Zumba that fateful Sunday morning and heard Twisted Sister's "We're not gonna take it!" something in me snapped. I wasn't going to take the drama anymore.

Within an hour, I had called a lawyer, found an apartment, hired movers, and began a new era of peace and rest.

I haven't screamed or yelled in two years, and I must tell you that this new way of being feels great. My happiness quotient. My creativity. My health. All have flourished exponentially since I decided to rest in peace.

Unrest Costs Too Much. You Can't Afford It!

There are times when I try on a blouse and like it. But then I look at the price tag and say, "I can live without it." Actually, when my budget is tight, I don't even go *into* certain stores. I know I'll be tempted to spend money I don't have.

I think we can all learn to be similarly as selective when we're talking about the peace in our lives.

Can the culprits of unrest and drama be avoided? When you enter a conversation and feel the turmoil rising – can you step away from the scene?

Guarding our inner peace is our job. No one and nothing can steal our peace. We *give* it away.

The expensive price of turmoil is that your judgment gets clouded. When our souls are at rest, our minds are clear, and we can approach the challenges of the day with clarity.

When we get "gotten" and open the door to agitation, all that is negative is amplified. The small matter that would normally be easily handled becomes monumental. Molehills become mountains. Emotional trenches are dug, and if we keep digging, we can feel like we're drowning.

The key is to nip negative momentum in the bud before the negativity builds into a full-blown meltdown.

How do you stop momentum?

Change the subject in your head or in your inter-personal communication. Do something completely different. Go for a run, or lose yourself in a good book. Follow a recipe, or sweat at the gym.

Or you could do my all-time favorite: nap.

A little siesta might just be the very thing to turn the tide and help you remember who you really are.

That you're really loved.

And that you love, too – deeply.

When gratitude fills your heart, you feel like YOU again.

With regard to stopping negative momentum, I'm not suggesting avoiding life or the big conversations that are necessary and important. But I propose that, for the sake of the peace in your heart, there are many people and topics that *can* be sidestepped and *should* be avoided.

Let the Arguments Begin!

I'm reading your mind right now. You're thinking about that one citizen that regularly shows up at your office door (or your inbox) and brings an arsenal of complaints.

If you were Mother Theresa, he'd *still* find fault with the way you help people. Further, you can't sidestep this person. It's your *job* to deal with the public – even the angry, unreasonable, unkind grouches that make you see red.

I chuckle remembering Paul Wilson (yes, his name has been changed for the sake of avoiding a nastygram). He was the *one* resident who would read our 300+ page budget document from cover to cover. He never missed a public meeting and never missed a chance to publicly point out even the smallest of errors.

My colleagues and I wondered if he had a life outside of finding fault with our work. I found myself re-reading every document to avoid the wrath of Mr. Wilson. My stomach was in constant knots.

Then I remembered, *I'm* the one in control of how I react to people and situations. I can't change Paul Wilson. But I can change the effect he has on me.

"When our souls are at rest, our minds are clear."

The decision to gracefully receive his input as a gift rather than a threat shifted the entire dynamic between us.

A good question to ask in these situations is, "Will this even MATTER in five years?" If it won't, and most things won't, then why give the anxiety and stress even five minutes of your beautiful today?

If you are spending time with people that are constantly draining your energy and resources, then maybe you need to take stock. If you are spending time with people that are takers and not givers, then think about the value you place on peace and rest. Start surrounding yourself with people who value peace too.

Peace is an inside job. Everything may be hitting the fan in your external world, but you can master the peace in your soul. Yes, this kind of internal peace takes practice. But you can do it.

Our Turtle likely had to retreat into her shell to silence the voices that said, "You'll never beat a hare."

Take comfort in knowing that peace isn't something outside of us that we need to try and grasp. Peace is not an elusive butterfly we hope will land on our shoulders. Peace resides *inside* of me and you. Peace is a flowing stream of well-being that we can tap into when we quiet our mind and emotions.

When you have all the feelings of being upset and in turmoil, take a five-minute break and BREATHE. Play some calming music, and remind yourself that you are connected to that source of peace.

You'll find getting a good night's sleep much easier too!

So, how good are you at sidestepping drama? Are you skillful or terrible at ignoring negative distractions?

On a scale of 1 – 10, how do you rate yourself on the level of Rest and Peace you have inside your heart and soul? Turn to page 152, and fill in your score.

"When gratitude fills your heart, you feel like YOU again."

TURTLE
Transparency

"If you tell the truth, you don't have
to remember anything."
– Mark Twain

We hear much about transparency as government employees. We know it is the government's obligation to share information with citizens. Government transparency holds officials accountable for the conduct of the people's business.

One of the solemn and agonizing duties of my role as a Public Information Officer was to respond to Open Records or Freedom of Information Act requests. Many of you reading this are nodding your heads because you know what it's like to have a full to-do list interrupted by a request for records that could take weeks to seek out and provide. The clock ticks loudly and, unless an extension is granted, you're on dead-line to respond.

We always coached our colleagues, "Don't put any information in an e-mail unless you want it on the front page of the paper." As a government employee, all communication is fair game. Transparency is the cornerstone of trust for public servants.

Transparency is also the cornerstone of trusting, healthy relationships in our personal and pro-fessional lives. And being transparent or clear, with no false fronts, will help you avoid burnout.

What Are We Afraid Of?

"Atelophobia" is the fear of not being good enough. The fear of not being perfect.

Transparency is removing the mask and reveal-ing who you really are. Transparency is getting beyond the surface to what is really going on in your heart.

If you are afraid of revealing your heart, afraid that your true self isn't good enough, you'll keep the mask on. And you'll never get to a juicy, fulfilling connection.

I encourage you to embrace your flaws.

Yes, you are flawed!

But you are awesome.

You're FLAWSOME.

And when you finally embrace your flawsomeness™, you are free to be authentically you in every situation which is just so nice. Being *you* takes far less energy than trying to be something or someone different.

Simon Sinek, a best-selling author and leading organizational consultant, captures this idea well: "To be authentic is to be at peace with your imperfections."

Own your flaws! Stop apologizing for being you!

How Do You Say "NO" Gracefully?

Just like the Fonz from Happy Days, who could

never admit he was wr...wr...wro...wrong, many of us in public service have a real problem saying "no."

Because you are big-hearted and so want to please, you can fall into the trap of thinking a "no" is a bad thing.

But an honest "no" can be your ticket to a much better day!

Try these on for size:

- No, for now.
- No, but here are some wonderful resources you may find helpful.
- No, but have you reached out to _____?
- No, I can't do that, but I CAN do this...
- Let me think about it.

If you want to say "no" but you feel stuck, that final, bulleted suggestion will always buy you some time. In every scenario, being strong enough in yourself to say "no" gracefully will win you respect. After all, you are the CEO of your life, your time, and your energy. Pretending to be Wonder Woman or Superman can garner momentary appreciation but is also the fast-track to burnout.

"Yes, you
are flawed!
But you are
awesome.
You're
FLAWSOME."

Let's go back to our friend, the Turtle. By all accounts, Turtle was a slacker. Her performance against the Hare looked pitiful. Couldn't Turtle have stepped it up a bit to at least keep up appearances?

I admire Turtle for embracing her flawsomeness. "Yep, I'm slow... but I'll get there. And I'll win the race not by performing for the crowd or pretending to be something other than turtle-like. I'll win by being myself."

Use Wisdom When Sharing

Transparency and honesty are intertwined, but let's add this caveat: use wisdom when sharing.

Salt is an amazing condiment. Just a little bit and all the flavors of that steak are amplified perfectly. A little too much salt? You want to spit that steak out, no matter how good a cut of beef you've grilled.

Truth, especially in a world of facades and posers, can be hard to take straight up.

Consider the recipient and consider *yourself*. How would *you* like to hear this information if the roles were reversed? A generous dose of empathy can perfectly season your foray into transparency.

If your truth is burning on your tongue and if you feel you'll burst if you don't speak your truth *now*, don't say it.

You've got so much emotion sandwiching your message, whatever you want to say will come out with spikes and edges that could damage your intent.

Like a good soup stock, let your truth simmer. Sift and sort until your message has clarity, devoid of too much passion. Then serve up your message when the timing is right. You wouldn't deliver a five-course meal to someone that just finished dinner, would you? Be strategic when delivering your message.

When I finally dropped the façade and started being real with people, I found they responded in kind. Shallow, superficial exchanges transformed into meaningful ones. The shift was kind of a relief! And we all got more done by being honest with each other.

"If you feel you'll burst if you don't speak your truth now, don't say it."

Have you established some relationships based on a flawed foundation of dishonesty? The kind where you say what you think others *want* you to say rather than what you really feel? You'll find these are the interactions that zap your energy the most and the very relationships you should begin shifting to transparency.

But What If...?

Every fearful thought begins with a "what if...?"

"What if I say no and [*worst possible scenario*] happens?"

Mark Twain understood the torment of a negative imagination when he said, "I've lived through some terrible things in my life, some of which actually happened."

The energy spent on imagining the worst-case outcome could be better spent processing your emotions, coming to clarity on your truth, and selecting the right time and place to deliver your message. If you're going to imagine, why not imagine an outcome that is *favorable*?

What if you say "no," and you DON'T have to take on that extra project?

What if you suggest a different way of doing something, and your idea is implemented?

What if you ask for that raise, and you get it?

Jack Canfield captured this idea well: "Everything you want is on the other side of fear." Don't expect fear to leave before taking action. Instead, use your fear as a springboard to get from where you are to where you want to be.

There's so much creativity, brilliance, expression, and wisdom just waiting to be unleashed in your life.

It's time to stop talking yourself out of speaking up.

On a scale of 1 – 10, how would you rate yourself on Transparency? Turn to page 152, and fill in your score.

"Use your fear as a springboard to get from where you are to where you want to be."

TURTLE
Levity

"Laughter is no enemy to learning."
– Walt Disney

On my very first day on the job as PIO, I was intent on winning over all 500 employees from the get-go.

As I walked through the parking lot toward the building, I saw my first opportunity to make a great first impression. The area was swarming with (mostly) men in bright colored vests. The Public Works guys! With all the energy and enthusiasm of a high-school cheerleader, I extended my hand to each of them (like a politician stumping for votes) and said, "Hi! I'm Brenda! Your new PIO!"

"If you can laugh at yourself, you put everyone at ease."

In my experience, Public Works employees aren't known for being the most boisterous, so I wasn't put off by the lackluster response. But I began picking up on some strange non-verbal cues.

There was a distinct look of horror on their faces. I looked around and then down.

Oh no!

I had walked my three-inch, spiked heels directly into their freshly poured concrete.

Putting aside my momentary distress at ruining my favorite pair of shoes and thoughts of how I could walk through the building of my new employer without a trail of wet cement following me, I knew this was a critical moment.

I could either burst into tears (which was quite a compelling course of action.)

Or I could crack-up and laugh.

Tears, while a viable option, tend to make everyone quite uncomfortable. Ah, but laughter?

If you can laugh at yourself, you put everyone at ease.

That day, I chose well. My laughter was contagious and instantly, I had twelve new friends.

A decade later, on my final day of employment with this township, these same Public Works' guys filled my office to say "goodbye." In a decade, we had shared many high and low notes. Babies had been born, parents had passed away, bridges had been built, and hundreds of potholes had been filled.

That's the beauty of public service. That depth of relationship is possible because so many of us are long-term co-workers.

Every single one of them said, "Remember that day...?"

How many dramas could we turn into comedy if we only add healthy doses of levity? Good humor builds bridges between people that are just as tangible as those made of brick and mortar.

Richard Scott, an American scientist and religious leader (two professions not necessarily equated with good humor), once said, "A good sense of humor is an escape valve for the pressures of life."

"Good humor

builds bridges."

Is your energy waning? Are you feeling like someone should stick a fork in you because you are DONE?

When was the last time you laughed?

Humor's Archenemy Is a Three-Letter Word

Ego.

As self-importance heightens, sense of humor diminishes. Often, those that are least likely to laugh at themselves are riddled with insecurities and doubts about their own self-worth. To compensate, they become larger-than-life, untouchable, and superior.

Ego says, "How dare you! Who do you think you are?"

Ego is touchy, easily offended, and often antagonized, insulted, and otherwise grumpy.

The greatest antidote for ego is levity. C'mon, lighten up! Is it the end of the world? Will what "it" is really matter five years from now? Can you find what's funny in moments of stress?

At this point in my live presentations, audience members clamor to share their memories. Once you get past the horror of the moment, there's plenty to laugh at.

From a live microphone worn into the bathroom stall to wardrobe malfunctions in public meetings, I could fill another book with the hilarity that goes on in government offices and school buildings around the country.

The person who taught me this lesson best? Our Township Secretary.

A legend in local government, even the meanest residents loved her. Why? Because she laced every conversation with hefty doses of good humor and was the first to laugh at herself.

Like the first evening meeting I attended as the Public Information Officer.

Except for August, most meetings were held in the Township Administration Building. A historic locale in one of our communities always hosted the August meeting – the final meeting before a glorious three-week summer break.

"As self-importance heightens, sense of humor diminishes."

The Secretary handled all the logistics and had a trunk full of awards to present to citizen volunteers. I arranged for the press to cover the festivities and had my trusty camera in hand to document the occasion.

Arriving with just a few minutes to spare, we rushed out of the car. Somehow, the doors clicked and locked with the keys still dangling from the ignition with all the awards still locked in the trunk.

We looked at each other with panic. An award-less disaster loomed.

A little nervous, but resilient as ever, the Secretary proved to be equally skilled at Teamwork. The Superintendent of Police and Chief Fire Officer were on speed dial. Within minutes, sirens screaming and lights flashing, help was on the way. The trunk released, and we sprinted into the meeting, juggling armfuls of awards as if heading to home base after rounding third.

Onlookers said it was the best meeting ever. Oh, but *we* knew. From that fateful evening on, we referred to each other as Lucy and Ethel. And we shared a good laugh about that meeting for years to come.

In most cases, the things that go wrong make the best stories. Think about a time when you could have crumbled and instead, you chuckled. Didn't that little laugh make everything better?

On a scale of 1 – 10, how would you rate yourself on Levity? Turn to page 152, and fill in your score.

"The things that go wrong make the best stories."

TURTL**E**
Encouragement

"I get by with a little help from my friends…"
– John Lennon and Paul McCartney

This survival guide implores you to not go it alone. Government work is not for the fainthearted! And certainly, it's best navigated in packs. It's a jungle out there.

Lucy had Ethel. Laverne had Shirley. Batman had Robin.

Who is *your* person? Or people?

Motivational speaker Jim Rohn famously said that we are the average of **the five people we**

spend the most time with. So, who's in *your* crew?

Take a moment and list the five people you spend the most time with:

1. _____

2. _____

3. _____

4. _____

5. _____

Now that you've made the list, what words best describe your people? Are they upbeat, energetic, resourceful? Or funny, insightful, and caring? Perhaps they are more like Eeyore than Tigger?

Are the words that best describe your people positive words or negative words?

If you're hanging around with whining, complaining, negative energy vampires, no wonder you feel like you're running on empty and feel like quitting!

Having the right or wrong people by your side via your phone, text, or e-mail can make or break you. Your people may be smarter, more experienced, or well-connected, but those aren't their best qualities.

Are they *encouragers*?

To encourage is to "give support, confidence, or hope to someone."

They give you courage to keep going. Courage is strength in the face of pain or grief. Courage is the ability to do something, despite feeling fear.

Isn't that what we *all* need? Some encouragement?

For decades, my posse of closest friends have never failed to get excited about my latest scheme, see the silver lining in a problematic situation, and cheer me on after I've fallen flat on my face.

Each friend has a completely different disposition. Each offers a safety net of love and kindness that has kept me from crashing and burning.

"Courage is strength in the face of pain or grief."

What does encouragement look like?

It could be wordless.

A simple, surprise cup of coffee delivered to your desk for a late afternoon pick-me-up.

A wink or thumbs up as someone passes your office.

Maybe encouragement is a nod of support when you make an important point at a meeting.

For our friend the Turtle in ***Aesop's Fables***, her friends cheered her on and kept her plodding toward the finish line. The cheers were so loud they actually woke the Hare up!

Maybe you're not hearing a cheering crowd, but smiles are a happy boost.

When people look genuinely delighted to see you, that delight can be an invisible nudge up-ward for your mood.

That's why I go to Bob's Cleaners.

The Dry Cleaners with Good Vibes

Any store can slap some inspirational quotes on the wall (see page 89). That doesn't determine the vibe.

The feeling comes from people and the energy they bring to a situation.

Enter the guy I always referred to as "Bob."

This is the ear-to-ear smile you will always get when you go to Bob's Cleaners. Even when I don't have dry cleaning, I'll stop by to say "hi." On a recent visit, I brought a friend (yep, this is

Bob's Cleaners

*This little outpost in the Gulf Gate section of
Sarasota is uncommonly encouraging.*

the kind of dry cleaners you'll bring a friend to) and excitedly introduced him to Bob.

Who politely said, "Actually *my* name is Craig."

Who knew?

The guy smiled so much you'd think he put the "Bob" in Bob's Cleaners.

A gentleman standing nearby with an armful of clothes said, "I drive through two towns just to come here."

People don't go out of their way for the dry cleaning (though the service is really good). That intangible "secret sauce" is about the feeling you get when you walk in the door. Businesses, churches, social clubs, households all have a vibe that comes from the people who energize them. Take stock of where you are spending your time and with whom you are spending your time.

Encouragement elevates you, like a hydraulic lift that lets you observe life from a higher vantage point.

"Encouragement elevates you."

We All Need Courage

Deliberately spoken words that say, "I believe in you," penetrate more deeply than chance encounters of commerce.

You may not have received those healing words from your mother or your father. But you can now choose who you surround yourself with to meet that deep need of the soul.

Everyone needs courage in this life. And everyone needs encouragers to help him or her rise up in the face of life's many fears.

And on those days when you feel like Tom Hanks in *Castaway*, be your *own* source of encouragement.

One of my favorite scenes from the hysterical TV series, *Parks and Recreation,* features the main character, Leslie Knope.

After a particularly long and grueling day in public service, none of her go-to people were available.

So, she picked up the phone and left herself a voicemail.

"Hey Leslie, it's Leslie. Hang in there. I love you. Bye."

Yes, you can always be your own best friend.

Do you encourage *yourself*?

Before you rate yourself on encouragement, I want you to consider the opposite. To be discouraged means you have become disheartened and lost confidence or enthusiasm. We'll talk more about that in the next chapter, but your enthusiasm level is a great indicator of how encouraged you are.

And that level is often determined by the thoughts you are thinking about yourself. When it comes right down to it, who *do* you think you are?

When you think about you, are your thoughts mostly negative or positive? Take a moment to think about your best self, and write an affirmation that reinforces all the good qualities you possess.

_____

_____

_____

_____

_____

_____

_____

_____

_____

Now take a moment and read your affirmation out loud. Did speaking it out loud feel weird? If so, you're likely not used to talking to yourself so kindly!

Now read it again. And again.

The more you read your kind affirmation, the more you'll believe it. Take the affirmation to a mirror and look at yourself as you speak kindly to yourself out loud.

Encourage yourself regularly and surround yourself with people who lift you up rather than drag you down.

On a scale of 1 – 10, how would you rate yourself on Encouragement? Turn to page 152, and fill in your score.

P.S. Now that you know who your encouragers are, take some time and call your people to thank them for being a bright spot in your life.

<u>H</u>ARE
Heart

"The miracle is not that we do this work,
but that we are happy to do it."
– Mother Theresa

As mentioned back in the Teamwork chapter, my cousin Pam is a special needs teacher in the public-school system. She received her Bachelor's degree and then a Master's in education. She is far more educated than many people working in the private sector for their six-figure-and-beyond salaries.

During a recent conversation, I was struck by her brilliance and insights on a variety of topics. The conversation veered to the struggle of raising children and pets while maintaining a household on her meager salary.

But then she talked about her "kids."

Oh, they're not her kids biologically, but boy, do they have her *heart*. Her eyes lit up when she talked about a letter she received. The letter was from a parent so grateful for the positive changes she's seen in her child. Changes that are a direct result of Pam's loving work.

Pam faces the school year knowing she won't have a budget for many of the items her classroom needs to thrive. So, she dips into her own, limited savings and makes certain there are enough crayons and scissors for little hands.

She doesn't do the work for the money or she would have left for greener pastures long ago. So too, would you.

The secret sauce that keeps you going long after many others would quit is heart. Your heart is where your love for the work resides.

Whether you're choosing a book for the entire community to read and discuss or repairing a bridge that thousands will safely traverse, your work as a public servant matters. Each time you painstakingly record the minutes of an important meeting or establish a new zoning ordinance, you are shaping and making history.

Teachers are shaping young lives. City administrators are shaping policy for future generations. Long after public servants retire, their work remains.

Theodore Roosevelt famously said, "Far and away the best prize that life has to offer is the chance to work hard at work worth doing."

Public service, government work, whatever you call it – it's work worth doing.

My Mom Loves to Iron. And My Dad...?

My father never made it past the eighth grade. Born to a farming family, he was needed in the fields rather than in the classroom.

His passion for all things mechanical led to tinkering with automobiles, racing stock cars, and driving a cement-mixer for his profession.

Each night, he'd arrive home and spend twenty minutes scrubbing his hands. Left unattended,

"Your heart is where your love for the work resides."

grease marks and caked on cement would make a lasting mark.

When overtime was available, he jumped at the chance because he valued taking care of his family. And each Sunday after church, he'd drive my mom, sister, and me to see what he'd built that week.

Whether he showed us the 34th Street Bridge leading into Ocean City, New Jersey or a new sidewalk surrounding a shopping center, he was proud of his work.

Heart is the motivation to work. When heart combines with performing work that matters to *you*, there's a joy – even in hard work – that is downright satisfying.

What's Your Motivation?

You probably have more than a few motivations, so take a minute and write down what motivates you:

1. _____

2. _____

3. _____

4. _____

5. _____

Now answer this honestly: does your work *matter* to you?

If the answer is "No" - Houston, we have a problem. Maybe the solution is to pivot toward an entirely new career.

But I'm betting those of you who cared enough to get a copy of the ***Public Servant's Survival Guide*** also care about your work.

Broader than the task-centered like/loathe list from our Teamwork Chapter, think about what matters to you about the work you do and why.

Let's write out a few:

1. _____

2. _____

3. _____

4. _____

5. _____

Remember, why work matters to *you* might bore someone else to tears. But that's why there's chocolate *and* vanilla.

So Why Did I Quit My Job in Public Service?

I eluded to the answer to this question in the introduction to this book. So, here's my true confession about why I left public service: I lost my heart for it.

Why?

My reason wasn't the constant scrutiny of citizens that didn't appreciate my hard work. Sure, there were a grumpy few, but by and large, the citizens of my community were wonderful.

My colleagues and I also survived a dark period when a few, vocal elected officials didn't value the professional staff. A grandstanding few found public fault-finding more expedient. We found ourselves uncomfortably in the hot seat and on the defensive during live, televised meetings. However, the majority of the elected officials I had the privilege to work for were amazing, brilliant, caring leaders who genuinely wanted what was best for their constituents rather than their political careers or party affiliations.

I started to lose heart when I lost the ability to grow and effect change.

Each year, I looked forward to the annual 3CMA (City-County Communications and Marketing Association) Conference. The conference was the one time of the year devoted to learning and expanding my profession as a Public Information Officer.

I'd submit work for awards consideration, sit in on sessions that inspired me, and I always brought back ideas to improve the quality of our government's communications.

Going to the conference was a relatively small expenditure in the budget. But the funding was cut.

This was also around the time that social media was emerging as a tool used by local govern-

"Heart is the motivation to work."

ments to effectively tell their stories and inform citizens about projects.

I wrote a stack of memos outlining the benefits while addressing the potential pitfalls of starting a township Facebook page and YouTube channel.

I can take "no" for an answer. Silence is far worse. When you feel like you are spinning your wheels and no one is listening, you can easily lose heart.

When you don't see a path forward for growth, you lose heart.

And as I said in the beginning of this book, far too many caring, talented, loyal public servants finally crash and say, "Enough!" For me, when I could no longer grow, I had to go.

Teamwork, Unity, Rest, Transparency, Levity, and Encouragement provide crucial fuel to keep you from running on empty. But losing heart? That's akin to blowing up your transmission.

Interestingly though, as I lost heart for public service, my heart for public servants grew. And out of that love, my passion to encourage amazing people like you was born.

So, If You've Lost Heart, How Do You Gain It Back?

Knowing that you have a problem is the first step toward your solution!

Your short temper, fatigue, lack of creativity, or overall malaise are symptoms.

Take some time to backtrack and unpack your emotions to pinpoint what caused you to lose heart. Because you're busy, a good amount of time may have passed from when you got off track to where you are today. And in that space of time, negative momentum grows.

Let's nip this negative momentum in the bud!

Reminding yourself about why you cared in the first place is a great starting point. What has changed since the beginning? Do you have a different manager? Has your job changed? Are there personal challenges impacting your professional energy?

"To get your heart back, you need to get hope back."

Talking about work/life balance is popular in these cases. Yes, balance is important, but we don't live two separate lives. We bring our work home even if we never check our computers. Projects and deadlines and budgets live in our hearts and our minds. We also carry our home life into the workplace. Being a parent or a caregiver to an ailing mother isn't something you can just place into a filing cabinet and pull out again when it's convenient.

We have one life and that life includes work and home and hobbies and a myriad of relationships that either drain or rejuvenate us.

Sometimes, a Problem Needs to Be Solved.

When you're not the only one losing heart, a larger issue is in play.

In one community with which I worked, a dark cloud descended over every department and division. Morale was at an all-time low, and even the best and brightest public servants were polishing their resumes and circulating them.

Why?

Everything rises and falls with leadership. This municipality had an administrator who ruled by fear and whose lack of personal integrity negatively impacted the entire workforce. The culture was toxic, and the pervasive feeling was of despair and futility.

After years of suffering in silence, a few respected members of the leadership team put their heads and hearts together and said, "This has got to stop." They gathered the facts, asked for a meeting with the elected officials, and took the risk to appeal for change.

And they got the changes they lobbied for.

The story has become legendary. The municipal board room featured a wall of windows covered by heavy curtains. The entire workforce - all 500 public servants - were uncharacteristically summoned for a special meeting.

The Board President walked to the wall of curtains and pulled them open. Sun streamed into the once-dark meeting room. And he said, "Today begins a new day."

The unsavory leaders had been terminated. And the rebuilding began.

Toxic cultures don't change overnight, but hope was birthed that day.

And to get your heart back, you need to get hope back.

On a scale of 1 – 10, how would you rate yourself on Heart? Turn to page 152, and fill in your score.

H**A**RE
Appreciation

"A person who is appreciated will always
do more than is expected."
– Unknown Author

Our Township's Employee Recognition program faced an uphill battle. Created to stimulate expressions of thanks and gratitude among team members, you'd think the program would be a smashing success. The problem? A pervasive feeling within the organization, generally sounding like, "Why should I say 'thank you' for the job you're *paid* to do?"

If pay was enough, many of us would never lose heart at work. Global studies reveal that 79% of people who quit their jobs cite "lack of appreciation" as their reason for leaving. I bet that number is similar for spouses who quit their marriages!

Private-sector companies, recognized as leaders in employee engagement, offer an array of benefits you'd *never* see in a government workplace.

On-site massages, beer coolers, meditation rooms – fuhgeddaboudit. Every penny spent in a government workplace is highly scrutinized, so building a culture that fosters appreciation takes creativity, frugality, and tenacity.

Our team was devoted to shifting the old, dusty, crankiness of our organization, and we eventually succeeded.

Soon, "Way to Go!" cards decorated cubicles in the library department as well as work areas in our machine shop. We held monthly drawings, rewarding both the givers and receivers of the cards. Saying "thank you" for a job well done became business as usual.

Appreciation fertilizes a happy workplace. And a happy life.

"Appreciation fertilizes a happy workplace."

How Do You Fertilize Your Life?

Let me take you back to a story from high school. It was love at first sight.

I was 16 years old. And no, I wasn't making eyes at the captain of the football team. I fell in love with a 1981 Chevy Camaro Berlinetta. This story, however, is NOT about a car.

Still, let me paint a picture for you. The car was a second-generation Camaro, the last model year with the rounded body style. It had black leather bucket seats, a sunroof, and silver pin-striping.

I have no idea what engine type was under the hood, but it didn't matter because the car had air conditioning and an 8-track player.

The Camaro beckoned to me from the show-room floor.

A confluence of miracles resulted in me driving that black Berlinetta out of the showroom. Certainly, my new car would solve my self-esteem issues, secure me a prom date, and send my classmates into a jealous frenzy.

None of *that* happened.

What *did* happen was the minute I drove that car off the lot, it **depreciated by 11%**. At the end of the first year, that depreciation percentage **rose to 19%**.

I learned the concept of DEPRECIATION.

Webster's defines "depreciate" as "to diminish in value over a period of time or to disparage or belittle." Depreciation shrinks things.

Which got me thinking about APPRECIATION.

Could it be said that appreciation *grows* things?

When I water and fertilize my flowers, they grow. Saying "thank you" or complimenting a friend grows a relationship. When I make deposits into my savings, that account grows. APPRECIATION is like a magical super-sizer.

"Acts of appreciation GROW things."

Famed inspirational speaker and motivational coach, Tony Robbins, defines appreciation this way: "Trade your expectations for appreciation and the world changes instantly."

Imagine that you're enjoying a walk down main street on a sunny, breezy day. The walk brings a smile to your face. You say to a passerby, "Isn't it a beautiful day?"

She agrees, smiling.

And your appreciation has made a beautiful day even better by the very act of appreciating it.

Conversely, when I throw a Burger King wrapper in my garden bed, the paper chokes the roots. If I don't tend to the weeds or protect my plants from critters or pests, they get eaten alive. When I neglect my garden, I am depreciating it.

Acts of appreciation GROW things.

Acts of depreciation SHRINK things.

So, What Happened to the Camaro?

Those first months of owning that gorgeous,

black Camaro were a honeymoon of high-octane gasoline, washing and waxing, and parking in remote locations to protect the car from dings.

A year later, I left for college. Juggling classes, homework, and a job to pay the bills left little time for fun. Late night pizzas and the endless dining hall buffet resulted in my packing on the freshman ten (well, twenty), and along with neglecting my body, my Camaro suffered.

I never got around to changing the oil. The car became a repository for fast food wrappers, dents, and parking tickets from Glassboro State College. A few years later, my Camaro died an early death on the highway, sputtering in contrast to its former glory.

Because of the way I *didn't* take care of the Camaro, it steadily diminished in value.

Had I appreciated it and cared for it, my gorgeous, black Camaro might be a classic today – the target of "oohs" and "ahhs" at car shows.

When we stop appreciating what we love about our lives, whatever "it" is depreciates. The best examples of active depreciation are the three "n's": nit-picking, negativity, and neglect.

"Appreciating what we have super-sizes what's good."

Conversely, appreciating what we have supersizes what's good.

Act Now to Appreciate Your Life.

How can we actively appreciate our lives? The first step is to acknowledge what is good, right now. So, do it! Make a list of positive aspects from your professional and personal life:

PERSONAL	PROFESSIONAL
1.	1.
2.	2.
3.	3.
4.	4.
5.	5.
6.	6.
7.	7.
8.	8.

The second step is to praise progress instead of lamenting baby steps. Don't forget to look over your shoulder and see how far you've already come! Stop complaining about what you didn't, should have, or might have done. The past is in your rear-view mirror. You're not going there.

My Camaro could be a tale of regret but regrets only serve to weigh us down. Instead, I appreciate the lesson learned and now choose to compliment, applaud, and tend to the things (and people) I value. I don't want to take the blessings of life for granted until they depreciate from view.

None of us choose government work to get rich. Public Service has its benefits, literally – but more often the work itself is what we love.

As mentioned earlier in the book, my father drove a cement mixer, and on Sundays after church, he'd drive us to see what he constructed that week. He passed away when I was just ten, but long after he was gone, my mom would take us to the beach for a week every summer. Each time we crossed the 34th Street Bridge in Ocean City, New Jersey, we thought, "Dad did this."

"Your work is your legacy. Appreciate it!"

There's pride and appreciation to be felt because of your children's story hours, new zoning districts, the graduates of your citizen's police academy, and the children taught to stop, drop, and roll. Your work is your legacy. Appreciate it!

I left the PIO's office almost a decade ago. But in the Township building is a huge mural that welcomes visitors to the second floor. Created to celebrate a landmark in our history, the collaboration with our local historical society remains today. This project took SO many hours to pull off, but when we unveiled the mural to the community (by now I had how to unveil things down pat), it was one of my proudest moments. And knowing that the mural will be there long after I am gone makes my heart happy.

Think about what you have contributed that will last far after your public service is done and you've headed into glorious retirement.

What are the stories you tell about your life?

Are you rehearsing the highs and minimizing the lows?

I bet Turtle enjoyed retelling her unlikely victory over the Hare. We have retold this fable for generations, and we still glean riches from the story.

Fertilize your life with appreciation, and watch it grow.

On a scale of 1 – 10, how would you rate yourself on Appreciation? Turn to page 152, and fill in your score.

HA<u>R</u>E
Reward

"Treat yo' self."
– Tom Haverford and Donna Meagle
from the TV Show, *Parks and Recreation*

In early 2009, the buzz around our municipal building surrounded a new TV show called **Parks and Recreation**. My colleagues and I rolled our eyes, bracing for a scathing parody of a public servant's life.

Oh, these characters were definitely silly but had undeniable heart. Amy Poehler as Leslie Knope embodied a passionate idealist with a vision to make a better world. Or at least, a better Pawnee, Indiana. Her line, "What I hear when I'm being yelled at is people caring loudly" became a go-to phrase to survive attacks by surly citizens.

An entire book of lessons on public service could be written from this brilliant series which ended in 2015. But one message that should not be overlooked is "Treat yo' self."

Tom and Donna, co-workers in the Parks and Recreation Department, established one day a year to do or have anything they wanted. On "Treat Yo' Self Day," selfishness reigned and was even celebrated. From renting a Bentley to spa treatments and purchases of fine leather goods, the glee the two expressed with each indulgence was palpable. One year they invited a downtrodden (but conservative) colleague to accompany them on their lavish escapade. He watched cynically as they shopped their way through the local mall, until finally they challenged him to *please* think of something to treat himself.

In the next scene, we see Tom and Donna's colleague wearing a full-blown Batman costume. A purchase that brought a tear to his eye and helped this city administrator reclaim his swagger.

"Treat Yo' Self" is an actual day observed by devotees of the show each October 13th.

When was the last time *you* "treated yo' self"?

Reward Is Not One-Size-Fits-All

It's six o'clock in the morning. My office is still shrouded in darkness. A steaming cup of really strong coffee sits to my right. Spa music plays on my Google mini. And I plunk, plunk, plunk at the keyboard, writing.

This "me" time is my reward.

I'm not writing a press release or a newsletter. I'm not building a marketing campaign or a social media post.

No, I am pouring my heart out over the latest lesson learned. To me, a self-avowed "word-nerd," finding language to perfectly describe my feelings is cathartic. Somehow, the written word makes sense of the jumble of thoughts in my head and brings clarity.

Writing is my reward.

My friend, Steve, the owner of several successful businesses, finds his reward on the links. Whether his round of golf is great or not isn't the point. Being on the course, surrounded by nature, his only companion for 18-holes is a blanket of quiet. This brings that same feeling of peace within himself that my keyboard time brings me.

Shirlee escapes the pressures of the day on her five-mile morning jog. (I get winded just typing that.)

Anita meditates. Judy paints. Eric surfs.

Mind you, I'll take tea at the Ritz or a hot stone massage any day! But reward doesn't have to pain my pocketbook.

What is your version of reward? Write down a few things that you can do for yourself to make yourself feel happy and loved:

1. _____

2. _____

3. _____

"Reward comes from a place of self-love that says, 'I'm worth it.'"

So Why Don't We Reward Ourselves?

Avoiding rewards isn't about being too busy. Or financially strapped.

American entrepreneur and author Ryan Blair famously said, "If it's important, you'll find a way. If it's not, you'll find an excuse."

So, is reward important to you? If rewarding yourself for a job well-done is important, you plan for it. Scheduling reward time makes the reward happen.

My favorite part of reward is that the reward is between you and you. Scheduling time for a reward doesn't require someone *else* to do for you. Reward comes from a place of self-love that says, "I'm worth it."

Which I believe is the underlying reason too many plow through from task to task and never stop to breathe, celebrate, and enjoy.

When you think of *you*, are you moved with compassion?

When you think of *you*, do you feel the tenderness of love and acceptance?

Can you acknowledge yourself and your worth?

If the answer is "no," I want to jump through the page and assure you, it is never too late to begin the greatest of love affairs.

With yourself.

May I gently ask you this question: can you look in the mirror and say unabashedly, "I LOVE YOU"?

Oh, at first loving yourself feels as uncomfortable as a nun walking into a biker bar.

But practice makes perfect.

Yes, you've failed. You've hurt and fallen short and had your heart broken and have broken a few hearts yourself.

You may be in a prison of your own making, punishing yourself for wrongs done or opportunities lost.

You may even have royally screwed up this thing called "life."

But right now, you are breathing.

"It is never too late to begin the greatest of love affairs. With yourself."

I encourage you to take every one of those per-ceived foibles, failures, and flaws and conjure up another F-word: FORGIVENESS.

If you keep making the same mistakes over and over or are hitting a wall repeatedly, I encourage you. Go back to square one. See yourself through eyes of compassion.

Conjure up LOVE when you see yourself in the mirror.

Some people may mistakenly label this message narcissistic or selfish. I choose to agree with au-thor Louise Hay, who said, "You've been criticiz-ing yourself for years and it hasn't worked. Try approving of yourself and see what happens."

You just might live happily-ever-after with the one person you are guaranteed to spend the rest of your life with.

YOU.

Kick Guilt to the Curb

Whoever came up with the phrase "guilty pleas-ures" took all of the fun out of them.

Guilt is a pervasive feeling in our culture, and yet guilt is a completely unproductive emotion if it doesn't provoke corrective action!

Must we feel bad to prove we care? Must we always be busy to prove we're committed?

Sorry, but life's too short to taint your pleasures with guilt.

Mind you, guilt can be a great barometer for change. If every time you uncork that bottle of red wine, you feel a twinge of guilt, that feeling could be your inner being saying, "Lay off the alcohol." If you've snapped at your spouse and feel guilty, an apology may be in order. Taking corrective action should release you from guilt. If the guilt lingers, that's self-abasement. And all that extra guilt accomplishes is misery.

I'm a late bloomer who has just discovered Downton Abbey. Downtime is Downton time as I binge-watch my way through the series.

This weekend, I sat immersed in the storytelling, thoroughly captivated by the escapism (and costumes!). Then I had a nagging thought: I should be doing something productive.

"Conjure up LOVE when you see yourself in the mirror."

"Life's too short to taint your pleasures with guilt."

I listened to the thought for a moment, then flushed it.

Yes, there are always productive things to be done. But must they get done?

Public servants work HARD.

Jim Rohn said it best: "By working hard you get to play hard, guilt free."

So now that we have made a case for Reward and uncovered its enemies – deficient self-love and abundant guilt – how would you rate yourself on Reward?

Turn to page 152, and fill in your score.

HARE

Evaluation

"Without proper self-evaluation,
failure is inevitable."
– John Wooden

You might think this is the part of the book where you tally up your scores from the previous chapters. Almost!

Before we go there, let's take a moment to look at the importance of evaluation in a balanced, happy life.

Too often we steamroll through our "to-do" lists and mark the calendar for weeks away, never considering the here and now. In this state of mind, we can easily veer an inch or two off course and, if left unchecked, eventually find ourselves miles away from our goal.

People burn out when they don't check in with themselves regularly.

Remember My 1981 Camaro?

I disregarded my check engine light for too long. The car eventually sputtered and died from neglect. And how much more valuable are *you* than a car?

No, you don't have a flashing hazard light that will blink you to attention (though that would be useful). But your behaviors are the signals that will warn you that you are teetering on the edge of burnout.

When your tank is full of Teamwork, Unity, Rest, Transparency, Levity, and Encouragement, you have the Heart to Appreciate your life and Reward yourself. When you're running on empty in any of these areas? You're impatient, grumpy, anxious, depressed, lacking in creativity and inspiration, and feeling overwhelmed. Songs like "Take This Job and Shove It" become your anthem.

But remember, your life is an inside job. This is between you and you. And as the CEO of your life, you owe it to yourself to evaluate regularly and course correct accordingly.

When *you* change, everything changes.

Heading a breakdown off at the pass is a great idea, but when you're not accustomed to tuning into your emotional guidance system, a full-fledged meltdown may occur.

Please don't beat yourself up for your melt-downs. This is just the universe's last-ditch effort to finally get your attention.

Extreme reactions or circumstances never fail to capture our attention. The tendency is to freak out or shut down. And you may. But as long as you eventually ask the question, "What's *really* going on here?" you'll get your answer.

Making it a regular – even daily – practice to check in with yourself and see how you're doing allows you to tune up rather than breaking down.

And if you break down? Breakdowns usually precede breakthroughs.

A Literal Break Down...

I had a project that was several years in the making. Rebuilding the small, historic bridge in our community disrupted everyone! No one likes detours, delays, or demolitions, and keeping citizens calm and informed about our progress was a full-time job.

That's why the ribbon-cutting ceremony for the new bridge was so important. By now, I had ribbon-cutting down to a science: write the press release, invite the dignitaries, set up the scene...

No longer new to the job, I had this down.

Celebrations are my favorite part of any job, especially when we can say we completed a project on time and under budget.

On the morning of the event, I left early for work. I adopted the practice of being first on the scene so I could set up the portable public address system and help everyone else find their places. A particularly grueling week was coming to an end, and I sang along with the radio with gusto.

Pop! Fizzle! Oh no!

"When you change, everything changes."

A flat tire timed disastrously.

Fear gripped me. Everyone will be in their places. The press will be there to record the proceedings.

And no one will be able to hear any of the announcements. Because the PA system was in my car.

This was long before Uber or Lyft, and in this part of town, taxicabs were non-existent.

Realizing the car would need to be abandoned for the sake of the greater good, I did the only thing I knew to do. I called the police.

Fortunately, my flat tire took place within the Township's borders, and a friendly officer picked me up, whisking me to the ribbon-cutting ceremony just in time.

I raced, wires flailing, to the assembly with PA system in hand. Frantically plugging in wires, I flipped the on switch and... feedback.

Not just polite squeaking. Full-on, plug-your-ears-because-it-sounds-like-the-apocalypse feedback.

When elected officials finally said, "Turn that thing off NOW!" I complied. And like a silent movie from the 30's, our bridge was officially reopened.

I held myself together on the ride back to the Township building with a colleague. Stoically, I headed straight for the third floor, walked into my office, shut the door, and collapsed into a heaving mess of tears.

After about 15 minutes, I heard a knock on the door.

It was one of the Commissioners. I had to respond.

My red nose and makeup trails from tears told the story.

"What's wrong with *you*?" she said, devoid of empathy.

"Well, the PA system…" I falteringly replied.

"Oh, get over it!" she interrupted. "If THAT's enough to get you this upset, you need to put your big-girl pants on."

"Breakdowns usually precede breakthroughs."

Pretending to pull myself together, I nodded in agreement. And after closing the door behind her, I dissolved into another puddle of tears. "Where is the humanity? Doesn't anyone care?" I cried.

What started with a flat tire gained momentum. Now my whole world was #$%@ed.

But she was right.

I had run on fumes for so long that when I needed resilience, charm, and good humor there was nothing from which to draw.

The well had run dry.

Had I been taking care of myself and checking my internal gauges, I still may have royally blown the event. But a loud PA system wouldn't have been the end of the world.

By the way, for any other Public Information Officers out there, PA systems (just like cell phones) often don't mix well with the building materials in bridges. Even if I had performed perfectly, the audio would have failed. Lesson learned!

Two Types of Decisions

Thought leader Simon Sinek says, "There are two types of decisions: good decisions and lessons learned."

If you learned something, the event wasn't a mistake.

Then why do you feel so bad?

Evaluate. Backtrack. Unpack the baggage you've built up over recent weeks.

Apply lavish doses of kindness to yourself.

The perspective of time makes a horror story your favorite to tell at that party a few weeks later.

Imagine our new friends, the Turtle and the Hare, regaling each other with the story of their first, legendary competition. Oh, what a lesson the Hare learned by napping in the middle of the race! And we tell their story to this day.

Evaluation and course-correction at regular intervals along life's way shortens the time it takes to go from despair to delight.

"If you learned something, the event wasn't a mistake."

So how good are you at evaluating your life? I hope much better after reading this book!

On a scale of 1 – 10, how would you rate yourself on Evaluation? Turn to page 152, and fill in your score.

Survival Guide Score

"Everything you don't know is
something you can learn."
– Unknown Author

U se this section to tally up your scores. As a reminder, ten means that you are a rock star, absolute perfection in this category. Zero acknowledges complete and utter failure in this category.

In most cases, you'll hover between four and seven, with one or two categories where you shine.

T – TEAMWORK   _____

U – UNITY   _____

R – REST _____

T – TRANSPARENCY _____

L – LEVITY _____

E – ENCOURAGEMENT _____

H – HEART _____

A – APPRECIATION _____

R – REWARD _____

E – EVALUATION _____

TOTAL: _____

Now that you have your individual scores and total score, let's look at where you are and what you can do to start raising your scores.

Remember, the goal is to constantly improve on where you are today, so your future is brighter and lovelier than your past.

First, based on your total score, place a checkmark where you landed:

[ ] 90 - 100

[ ] 80 - 90

[ ] 70 - 80

[ ] 60 – 70

[ ] Under 60

If you scored between a 90 – 100, why are you here? You should be writing this book! Now subtract 5 points for smugness. (Only kidding!)

If you scored between an 80 – 90, you have a healthy level of self-awareness and are probably one pedicure or a round of golf away from being refreshed to go the extra mile.

If you scored between a 70 – 80, schedule a night out with your best friends and get a good night's sleep. Immediately!

If you scored between a 60 – 70, then stop trying to be Wonder Woman or Superman! You need help, some go-to people, a vacation, and probably a martini or a huge cookie.

If you scored under a 60, then you need a hug and possibly a visit to the emergency room. Or a vacation. Start taking care of YOU.

Next, based on your individual scores, use the space below and answer the following questions:

What are your three top categories?

1. _____

2. _____

3. _____

What are your three lowest categories?

1. _____

2. _____

3. _____

I recommend taking a moment here and reflecting on both categories. First, what can you do to celebrate and reward yourself for scoring so high on your top categories?

Second, the point isn't to feel badly about your low-scoring categories. Instead, consider this a victory! You can't fix something if you're not aware it's a problem.

Use the following information as a guide to help raise your individual scores, so you can bump up your total score and live a more balanced, stress -free life.

Teamwork – Be curious! Have deeper conversations with the people you interact with, and find out what THEY love and loathe. Consider offloading some projects so you can spend time working on what you love and what lights you up.

Unity – Give your feelings some space to be heard. Don't just plow through a bad day. Care enough about how you are feeling to stop and consider why you feel the way you do. Brightening your day could be as simple a correction as getting something to eat!

Rest – Allot some time to unplug and refresh. "Rest" doesn't mean you have to sleep (though a nap is always a great idea). Simply take a break from electronics, or put a "Do Not Disturb" sign on your office door so you get a much-needed rest from interruptions.

Transparency – Consider the relationships or interactions that drain you most. They very well may be the relationships in need of a new level of honesty. Give yourself permission to speak your truth tempered with kindness and professionalism.

Levity – The next time you are inclined to frustration, anger, or despair, challenge yourself to find the funny. Jumpstart your sense of humor by watching a hilarious show (I recommend **Parks and Recreation** or **Schitt's Creek**), and embrace opportunities to laugh at yourself. Your laughter will be contagious.

Encouragement – Invite people into your circle who are up-lifters! The best way to attract them is to be an up-lifter too. You'll find if you look for opportunities to encourage someone else, you'll feel better already. And when no one is available? Look in the mirror and remind yourself that you're amazing. You've surmounted challenges before, and you've got this one too.

Heart – Go back to why you cared in the first place. Heart is often lost because we are caught up in projects and not in people. Remember why you love – or used to love – the work, and spend more time considering those things rather than the complaints that have risen up like weeds to choke your joy.

Appreciation – There's always something to be grateful for. Are you fertilizing your life and your job by acknowledging what's good? Putting the spotlight on the negatives won't serve you or help the situation. Change the stories you tell. Amplify the positive aspects. Rehearse them!

Reward – Treat yo' self! Whether you have ice cream for dinner, go for a walk in the park, or you immerse yourself in a good book, be good to yourself. Life is too short to fast forward from day to day without stopping to smell the roses. If our jurisdictions have ribbon-cuttings and grand openings to celebrate success, shouldn't we also stop to recognize that we've done well?

Evaluation – Which you've just done by reading this book. Good for you! This ***Survival Guide*** is intended to be your guide for future evaluation too. Every now and then take a step back and consider how you're doing. And adjust your course accordingly.

Your Next Steps

"What we learn with pleasure we never forget."
– Alfred Mercier

Congratulations on making it all the way to the end of this book! That you even started signals a commitment to personal and professional growth. You've followed through, and you should be proud of yourself.

Now, take the time to put everything you learned in this book into motion. I know that we've covered a lot, so you may feel a bit overwhelmed. But before we end, let me give you a few recommendations.

First, let what your scores revealed settle in and feel your feelings.

Second, pick one category and give yourself a specific action item to complete this week. Continue moving forward on that one category until you feel you've moved the needle. Then, choose a specific action item for another category you'd like to improve and continue the process.

Last, share what you've learned to encourage someone else.

If I were starting all over again, small action items and sharing is exactly where I would start. Can you do more? Of course, you can! But don't let your perfectionism get in the way of your progress. Remember that you're awesome, but you're flawed. You're flawsome! And you should Embrace Your Flawsomeness™.

Finally, I strongly encourage you to go to my website, www.meseminars.com, and download your free "ME-Book." This guide will jumpstart this love affair I'd like you to have with the one person you are guaranteed to spend the rest of your life with. You!

And for extra encouragement? Every two weeks, I pick a word and record a short inspirational video to inspire insights and fuel joy. You can find hundreds of these videos on a host of motivational subjects on my Facebook Page (www.facebook.com/BrendaViola722) or receive these posts directly to your email inbox by signing up for my semi-monthly blog posts.

Or, walking through the ***Public Servants' Survival Guide*** with you and your team live and in person would be my greatest pleasure. There's nothing like the energy of a group with shared stories and experiences to make this material come alive in a special, life-affirming way.

I know you can do it! You now have the game plan.

This world needs your gifts and talents – and most of all, the heart you bring to public service.

Thank you for all you do. Your work really does make a difference.

Looking for a Speaker Who Can Connect with Everyone in Your Audience?

Then look no further!

Brenda Viola will engage your audience with her energy, insights, and laugh-out-loud wisdom. Brenda's most popular topics include:

- Mastering the Media to Tell Your Story Effectively
- The Fear Factor: Facing Down the Bully to Realize Your Dreams
- Create Your Life, One Thought at a Time
- From Toxic to Terrific: How to Shift Your Corporate Culture
- Embrace Your Flawsomeness® and Kick Perfectionism to the Curb

Brenda is available for both live and online events. She will give your audience members valuable insight and actionable takeaways that they can use immediately.

Book Brenda today by contacting her at Brenda@MESeminars.com or 1.833.MPOWERME (1.833.676.9763)

See What Other Event Planners Have Said About Working with Brenda Viola:

"Brenda has a genuine ability to connect with audiences, and her messages are refreshing, thought-provoking, and meaningful. She has a high standard of professionalism that earns Brenda rave reviews at our international conference. I especially value her high standards and exceptional communication skills, which makes working with her such a breeze."

- Ashley DiBlasi
Asst. Director of Professional Development,
International Institute for Municipal Clerks

"Brenda is a highly energetic, compassionate, and knowledgeable presenter. She brings her own life experiences and insights as examples to the training table, inspiring others to dive into the realm of self-exploration. I highly recommend Brenda."

- Pamela Miller
Miller Management and Consulting Group

"Brenda did an excellent job starting off the second day of our Wild Wisconsin Winter Web Conference. Her presentation was well received by our librarians. She brings energy and passion to her presentations, and she was a joy to work with. I would absolutely hire her again! "

- Jamie Matczak
Education Consultant, Wisconsin Valley Library Service

About the Author

A unique heart for public servants is the springboard from which Brenda Viola teaches. With a
24/7 news cycle and demands to effectively
communicate impacting every branch of municipal work, "Mastering the Media" became the
cornerstone of Brenda Viola's training work.
Her gift to encourage and inspire led to the evo-
lution of ME (Municipal Education) Seminars
which combines professional skill development
and personal growth initiatives.

Armed with a Communications degree from Rowan University, experience as a news anchor and reporter, and a brief stint as a QVC Show Host, Brenda stepped into the government sector as a Public Information Officer in 2001. Her award-winning service for a first-ring suburb of Philadelphia lasted a decade. Her passion to support firefighters led to the creation of a scholarship program for students who volunteered with the Main Line area's fire companies.

As the Director of Marketing and Communications for a *Fortune*-ranked Best Small Business in America, she finds fulfillment in promoting products and services that make life better for thousands each year.

When she's not speaking at a conference, hosting a webinar, or posting inspirational messages on her 10,000+ member Facebook page (@BrendaViola722), she's singing bad karaoke at the Gulf Gate Moose Lodge in Sarasota, Florida where she resides. Brenda soaks up the year-round sunshine, enjoys a close-knit community of good friends, and relishes downtime to enjoy a good book or don her helmet to join her favorite guy, Mark, on his Harley Davidson.

Made in the USA
Middletown, DE
04 February 2021

33086143R00102